Fashion Coloring Book For Girls:

A Coloring Book For Girls of All Ages with Cute Fashion Style & Designs

SS Publications

THIS BOOK BELONGS TO

_____

_____

_____

I ♥ shopping

Conclusion

Thank you so much for purchasing this book. If you enjoyed it, then please leave an Amazon review. Reviews are the lifeblood of our publishing endeavors- leaving a positive review would mean the world to us.

Thanks a lot !

- SS Publications

Made in United States
Troutdale, OR
01/16/2024

16962846R00071